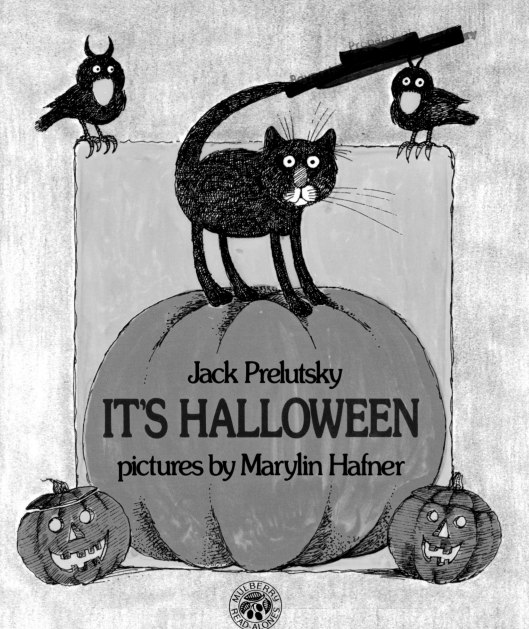

Jack Prelutsky

IT'S HALLOWEEN

pictures by Marylin Hafner

A MULBERRY PAPERBACK BOOK
New York

The Library of Congress has cataloged the
Greenwillow Books edition of It's Halloween as follows:
Prelutsky, Jack. It's Halloween. (Greenwillow read-alone book)
Summary: Thirteen Halloween poems for beginning readers.
ISBN 0-688-80102-1 ISBN 0-688-84102-3 lib. bdg.
1. Halloween—Juvenile poetry. [1. Halloween—Poetry]
I. Hafner, Marylin. II. Title. PZ8.3.P9It3 811'.5'4 77-2141

5 7 9 10 8 6
First Mulberry Edition, 1996
ISBN 0-688-14733-X

CONTENTS

MY
GLASS
IS
RUN
HERE

IT'S HALLOWEEN

It's Halloween! It's Halloween!
The moon is full and bright
And we shall see what can't be seen
On any other night:

Skeletons and ghosts and ghouls,
Grinning goblins fighting duels,
Werewolves rising from their tombs,
Witches on their magic brooms.

In masks and gowns
we haunt the street
And knock on doors
for trick or treat.

8

Tonight we are
the king and queen,
For oh tonight
it's Halloween!

SKELETON PARADE

The skeletons are out tonight,
They march about the street
With bony bodies, bony heads
And bony hands and feet.

10

Bony bony bony bones
with nothing in between,
Up and down and all around
They march on Halloween.

THE TRICKSTERS

Three Halloween tricksters are we—

My sister, my brother and me.

We roam through the streets

Playing tricks, getting treats —

Three Halloween tricksters are we.

Sister's a witch dressed in black,

Brother wears bones front and back,

I'm a ghost with no face

In an old pillowcase—

Three Halloween tricksters are we.

We are scary as scary can be—

My sister, my brother and me.

We frighten each other,

We even scare mother—

Three Halloween tricksters are we.

PUMPKIN

We bought a fat
orange pumpkin,
The plumpest sort
they sell.

We neatly scooped

the inside out

And only left

the shell.

We carved a funny

funny-face

Of silly shape

and size,

A pointy nose,

a jagged mouth

And two enormous eyes.

We set it in a window

And we put

    a candle in,

Then lit it up

    for all to see

Our jack-o'-lantern grin.

COUNTDOWN

There are ten ghosts
in the pantry,

There are nine
upon the stairs,

There are eight ghosts
in the attic,

There are seven
on the chairs,

There are six
within the kitchen,

There are five
along the hall,

There are four
upon the ceiling,

There are three
upon the wall,

There are two ghosts
on the carpet,
Doing things
that ghosts will do,
There is one ghost
right
behind me
Who is oh so quiet . . .

TRICK...

The people in this house were mean
When we asked for a treat.
They did not give us anything
And chased us down the street,

And so we soap
their windows
And so we chalk
their door

And so we think

    they'll never be

So nasty

    anymore.

THE GOBLIN

There's a goblin as green
As a goblin can be
Who is sitting outside
And is waiting for me.
When he knocked on my door
And said softly, "Come play!"
I answered, "No thank you,
Now please, go away!"

But the goblin as green

As a goblin can be

Is still sitting outside

And is waiting for me.

Give us candy,
give us cake,
give us something
sweet to take.

37

BOBBING FOR APPLES

Watch us bobbing for an apple,

For an apple apple apple,

But no apple apple apple,

Not an apple can I get.

Oh I cannot catch an apple,

Not one apple apple apple.

Though my sister got an apple,

All I got was soaking wet.

HAUNTED HOUSE

There's a house
　　upon the hilltop
We will not go inside
For that is where
　　the witches live,
Where ghosts
　　and goblins hide.

Tonight they have
their party,
All the lights are
burning bright,

44

But oh we will not

go inside

The haunted house tonight.

The demons there are whirling
And the spirits swirl about.
They sing their songs to Halloween.
"Come join the fun," they shout.

But we do not want to go there
So we run with all our might
And oh we will not go inside
The haunted house tonight.

BLACK CAT

A cat as black

As blackest coal

Is out upon

His midnight stroll.

His steps are soft,

His walk is slow,

His eyes are gold,

They flash and glow.

And so I run

And so I duck,

I do not need

His black-cat luck.

GHOST

I saw a ghost
    that stared and stared
And I stood still
    and acted scared.
But that was just
    a big pretend.

        I knew that ghost . . .

. . . it was my friend!

53

HAPPY HALLOWEEN

It's late and we are sleepy,
The air is cold and still.
Our jack-o'-lantern grins at us
Upon the window sill.

We're stuffed with cake and candy
And we've had a lot of fun,
But now it's time to go to bed
And dream of all we've done.

We'll dream of ghosts and goblins
And of witches that we've seen,

And we'll dream of trick-or-treating
On this happy Halloween.